Essential Ikebana

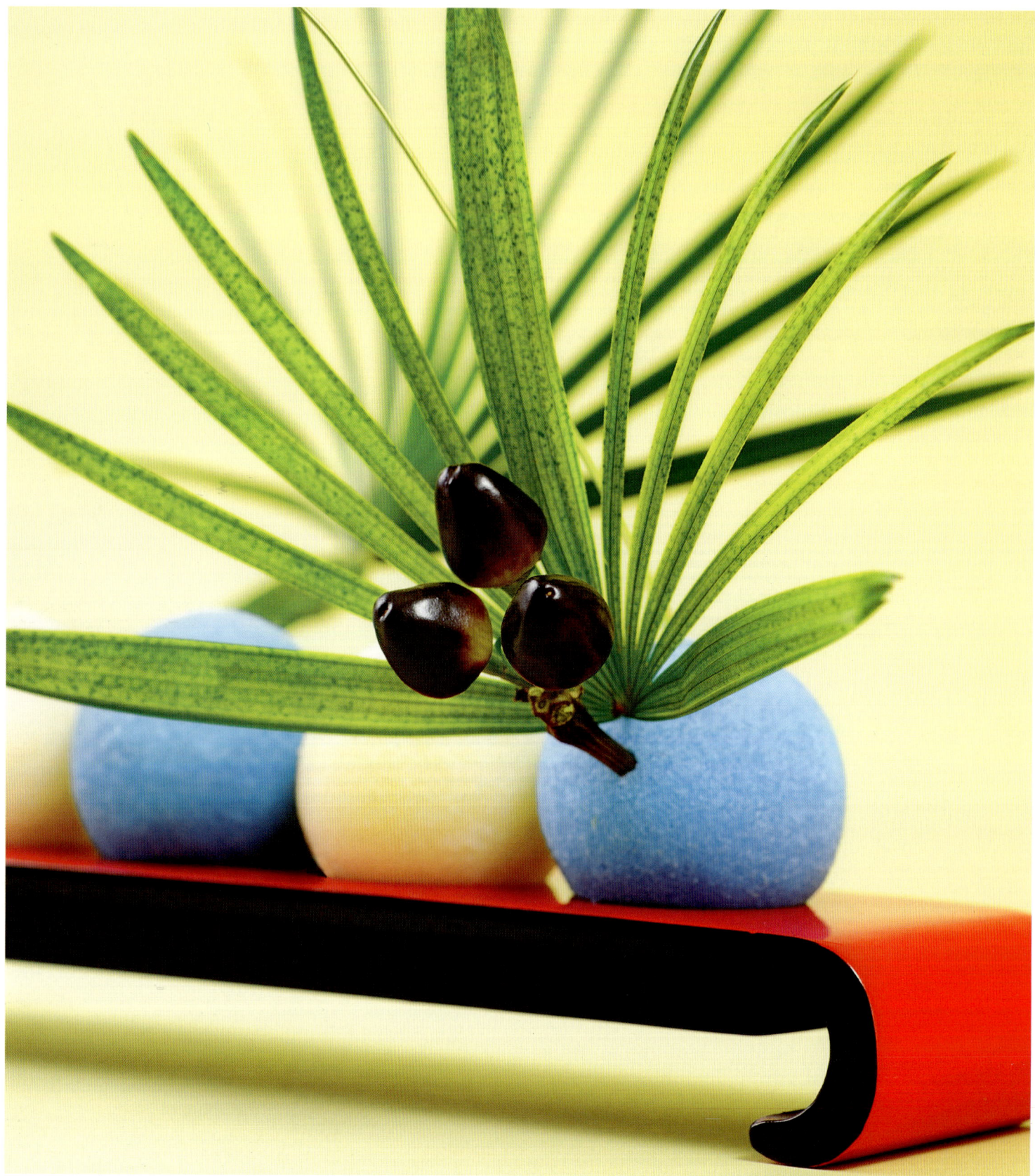

Essential Ikebana

Leonard Lim

mc Marshall Cavendish
Editions

Some of the content in this book was previously appeared in *Experiencing Ikebana* published by Times Editions.

Editor: Melvin Neo
Designers: Bernard Go Kwang Meng & Lynn Chin Nyuk Ling
Photographers: Edward Hendricks & Sam Yeo

Published by Marshall Cavendish Editions
An imprint of Marshall Cavendish International
1 New Industrial Road, Singapore 536196

Other Marshall Cavendish Offices
Marshall Cavendish Ltd. PO Box 65829, London EC1P 1NY, UK • Marshall Cavendish Corporation. 99 White Plains Road, Tarrytown NY 10591-9001, USA • Marshall Cavendish International (Thailand) Co Ltd. 253 Asoke, 12th Flr, Sukhumvit 21 Road, Klongtoey Nua, Wattana, Bangkok 10110, Thailand • Marshall Cavendish (Malaysia) Sdn Bhd, Times Subang, Lot 46, Subang Hi-Tech Industrial Park, Batu Tiga, 40000 Shah Alam, Selangor Darul Ehsan, Malaysia.

Marshall Cavendish is a trademark of Times Publishing Limited

National Library Board Singapore Cataloguing in Publication Data
Lim, Leonard, 1963-
Essential ikebana / Leonard Lim. – Singapore : Marshall Cavendish Editions, c2009.
p. cm.
ISBN-13 : 978-981-4276-52-8 (pbk.)

1. Flower arrangement, Japanese. I. Title.
SB450
745.92252—dc22   OCN456505331

Printed in Singapore by KWF Printing Pte Ltd

Contents

7   Preface

8   Acknowledgements

11   Introduction: Rikka, Shoka, Jiyuka

18   Getting Started: Cutting Stems,
Absorbing Water, Bending and Shaping Stems,
Basic Wiring Techniques, Holding Stems

28   The Fundamental Considerations:
Colour, Shape, Quality

36   The Materials: Accessories, Vases, Equipment

47   Freestyle in Three Movements: Vertical,
Horizontal, Slanting *(Step by step arrangements)*

58   Seeing in New Light: Line, Surface, Point, Mass
(Step by step arrangements)

84   Any Vase Will Do *(Step by step arrangements)*

98   That Special Moment *(Step by step arrangements)*

108   Right At Home

120   Till Then

Preface

To the uninitiated, ikebana is probably the placement of just a few flowers and leaves in a vase. Rigid rules, based on tradition and philosophy, govern the way these mere few stems are arranged.

While there is some truth in this perception, ikebana is much more than this. It is about our relationship with nature that takes us on a journey of discovering beauty in our hearts as we create beautiful ikebana. As we enhance the beauty of the natural flora and fauna in ikebana, our lives are, in turn, enriched. The process of ikebana is one filled with fun and adventure as we realize how rich and diverse are the offerings that nature has in store for us.

This book marks a new milestone in my journey in ikebana. It is based on my experience with Ikenobo ikebana since 1989, and that of my teachers' and their teachers'. I will introduce ikebana in a simple manner, and guide you through your first lessons in Ikenobo freestyle. My reward in this exercise is that you will be inspired to embark on and further your experience in ikebana. Each new encounter with ikebana, I hope, will be an invitation for all, including yourself, to see the beauty in you!

Acknowledgements

I would like to record my deepest admiration and gratitude to Ikenobo Sen'ei, 45th Generation Ikenobo Headmaster and Ikenobo Yuki, 46th Headmaster Designate for their vision and wisdom in sowing interest in ikebana in Singapore and their unfailing support and encouragement in my journey in Ikenobo ikebana.

Without the continued guidance and inspiration of all my Ikenobo teachers in Japan, invaluable exchanges with my students and colleagues in ikebana from all over world and the love and understanding of my family and close friends, I would not have had the opportunity to develop my love for Ikenobo ikebana to what it is today. Violet, Melvin, Lynn, Bernard, Sam and Edward—thank you for making this book a beautiful reality.

The Publisher and Author would like to thank M Hotel Singapore and Singapore Marriott Hotel for the use of the suites during photography, and Charles Lai, Joyce Yao and Xanthe Chan, for facilitating the arrangements.

Introduction

Ikebana is the Japanese art of flower arrangement. Ikebana is derived from two Japanese words, *ikeru* meaning "to arrange" or "to put life into" and *hana* meaning "flower". Hence, the central theme in ikebana is life.

The practice of ikebana is associated with Buddhism and *kuge*, the practice of making religious floral offerings, probably dates back to the sixth century. Ono no Imoko, a member of the royal family, was sent to China as Japan's first foreign envoy to study the customs and practices of mainland Asia. Upon his return, various cultural practices were readily absorbed into Japan, including Buddhism. Ono no Imoko was eventually ordained as a Buddhist monk and took on the name of Senmu Ikenobo. He thus became the first in a long line of Ikenobo headmasters famous for their wisdom and skill in ikebana. His descendants were also to succeed him as the head priest of the Rokkakudo temple in Kyoto which still stands today as an important landmark of Buddhism and the birthplace of ikebana. Ikenobo is regarded as the origin of ikebana and there are by now more than 3,000 schools of ikebana in Japan.

Over the years, the practice of ikebana has become acknowledged as one of the traditional Japanese arts and appreciated for its exquisite beauty. A few distinct styles of arrangement ranging from the traditional to the very modern and avant garde have evolved in the long history of Ikenobo and they can be broadly classified as rikka, shoka and jiyuka (freestyle).

Rikka

A very traditional and grand arrangement, rikka expresses the beauty of a natural landscape through the use of several different types of materials. Rikka had its beginnings in the *tatehana* ("standing flower") style of the 16th century. During this period, arrangements were constructed on a grand scale to adorn the huge halls in the mansions of the wealthy upper class that included the feudal lords and the samurais. Apart from the wealthy, the learned, including monks, were practitioners of ikebana. Women were then not allowed to practise ikebana.

This style is still being arranged with as much zeal today although it has now taken on a modern form and the size of the arrangements has become modest to fit new living environments.

A more dramatic, new version of the rikka style was introduced by the current 45th Ikenobo Headmaster, Ikenobo Sen'ei in April 1999.

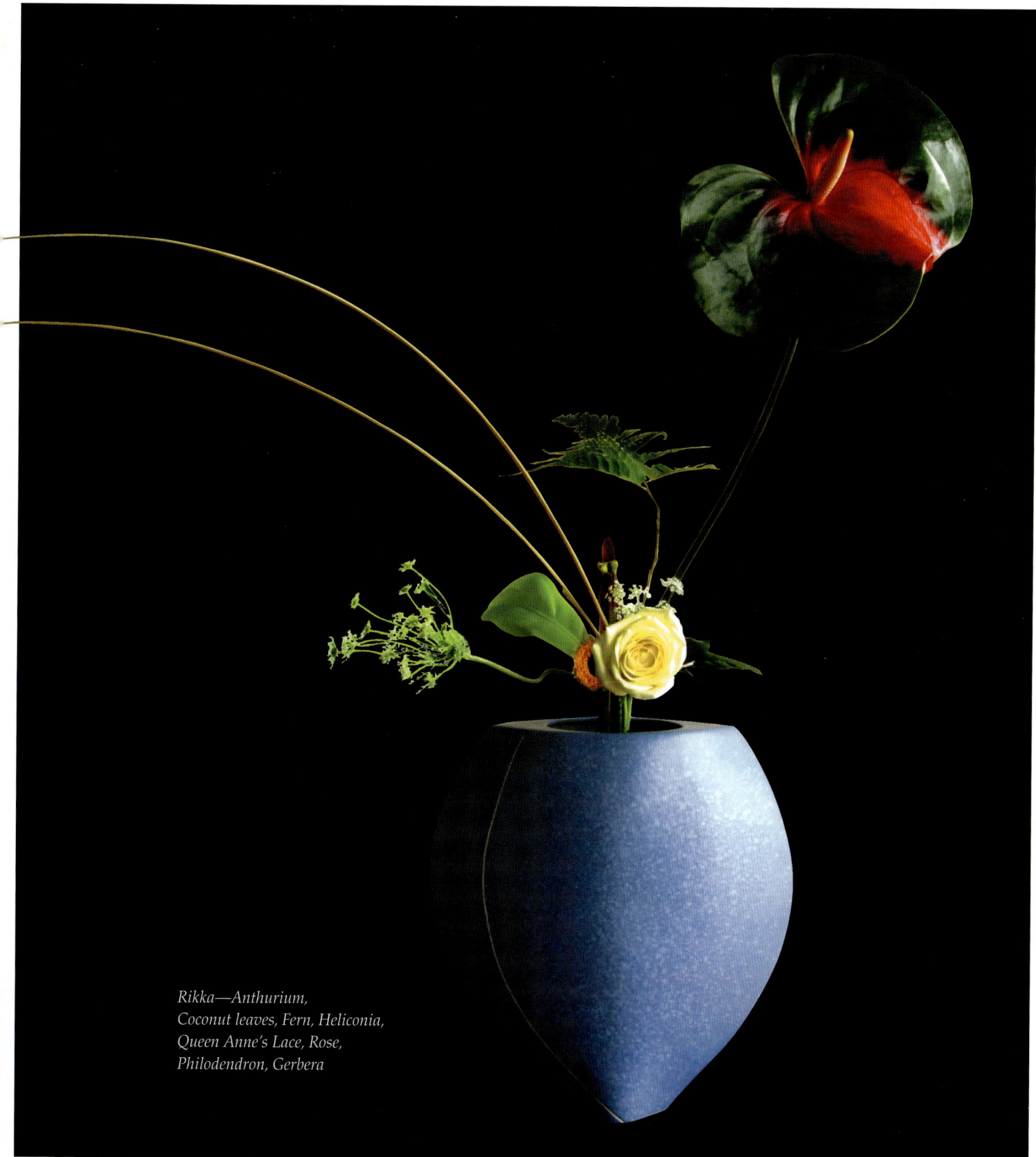

Rikka—Anthurium,
Coconut leaves, Fern, Heliconia,
Queen Anne's Lace, Rose,
Philodendron, Gerbera

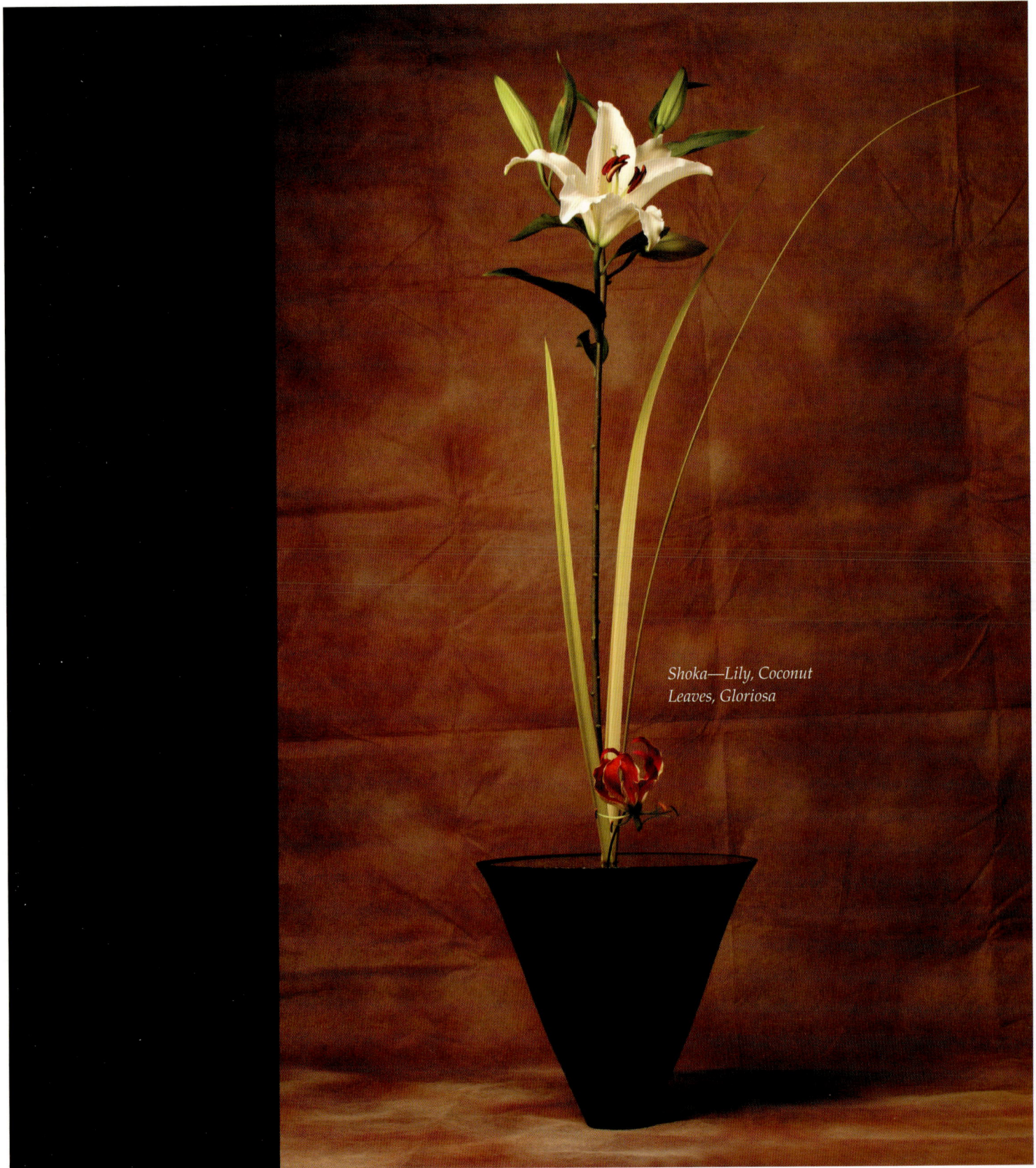

*Shoka—Lily, Coconut
Leaves, Gloriosa*

Shoka

Simplicity and elegance would best describe shoka. Shoka focuses on the beauty of the natural form of plants. Up to three different types of materials are used in shoka arrangements.

The style dates back 200 years to a time when ikebana became popular with the middle class and they began to arrange ikebana in their homes.

Shoka is traditionally placed in a special alcove called a *tokonoma*. As the homes of the middle class were smaller, the size of ikebana arrangements was scaled down to fit the *tokonoma*. This was the era when women started to study and practise ikebana.

Changes to the architecture of the modern Japanese home, new ideas in aesthetics and the influx of new, foreign, exotic floral materials into Japan are among the major reasons for the evolution of a more modern version of the traditional shoka style introduced in 1977 by the current 45th Ikenobo Headmaster.

Jiyuka (Freestyle)

This is the most recent style to evolve, displaying exciting diversity in creativity and the virile imagination of the individual.

There are two faces to this style—the naturalistic and the abstract.

In the naturalistic form, the beauty of the floral and branch materials takes centrestage. Materials are used as they are in nature, without any modification. The harmonious selection of materials is freely arranged to display inherent beauty. In the abstract form, certain aspects of the materials are highlighted so as to discover a newfound beauty. The purpose is to provoke a sense of delightful wonder and amazement.

In the following pages, you will discover the numerous possibilities in freestyle and it is only the beginning of your fun-filled journey in freestyle!

Freestyle—Phalaenopsis,
Yellow Phoenix, Money Plant,
Plastic Gardening Mesh

Getting Started

Cutting Stems

Cutting of materials is done with ikebana scissors known as *hasami*. This is done by placing the stem at the base between the blades and closing one's grip to complete the action. Thicker and harder stems will require making a few initial shallower cuts before the final cut. As the *hasami* comes in various sizes, it is important to select one that provides a comfortable grip.

The Bare
Essentials in a
Nutshell

Absorbing Water

This process is crucial to all floral materials. Employing the correct technique to ensure efficient water uptake will allow your arrangements to be enjoyed for a longer time. Knowing the flowers' drinking habits will also help you to preserve the arrangements longer.

The most common and effective method is to cut the stem under water as this prevents air from entering the stem which would then block its water uptake. Change the water in the arrangement and make fresh cuts every few days or when the water begins to smell or turn murky.

Another common method is to add chemicals to the water in the vase. Commercial preparations of "plant food" solution are readily available. These enhance water uptake as well as keep the water in the container clean and bacteria-free. Aspirin, vinegar and peppermint oil are among some other common chemicals that can be used.

Other methods include charring the freshly cut surface over a flame or soaking the freshly cut surface in boiling water. Stems that leak out sappy fluid can be crushed and have salt rubbed in to open the water channels so that water uptake can take place. Another alternative is to use a special flower pump to force water into the hollow stems of materials like the lotus.

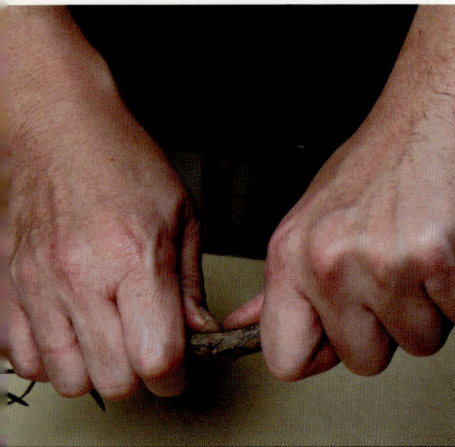

Bending & Shaping Stems

While cutting and trimming the branches of a stem may give the desired line and curve, quite often the stem has to be bent and shaped to achieve this. The action is considered a success only when the stem remains curved.

For thin, leafy materials and stems of moderate thickness, placing them between the finger and thumb and gently drawing them along will give them a nice curve. Varying the pressure is necessary so as not to damage the leaves and stems.

The two thumbs should be placed as close as possible together to control the pressure. As my teacher always cautions, stop before the stem snaps!! One useful tip is to "warm" the stem in the palms first. This makes the stem more supple and pliable before bending and reduces the risk of breaking it into two.

For woody branches, it is necessary to make a superficial, diagonal cut on the stem before using the thumbs to bend the branch. A cracking sound is usually heard which indicates that the action is about complete.

When all else fails, wires can be secured to the stem or inserted (for example, with hollow stems) so that the stem can be bent easily. Avoid excessive wiring—use only as much as is needed. Camouflage the wires with floral tape as, otherwise, they will stand out in the completed arrangement.

Wires are not permitted in shoka arrangements.

Basic Wiring Techniques

EXTERNAL WIRING I

A piece of wire, of a suitable thickness, is placed alongside the stem. The length of wire should be able to support the weight of the material and be longer than the part of the stem to be bent. One end of the wire is then wound in big loops to secure the supporting wire to the stem. Camouflage the wire by wrapping it with matching coloured floral tape. At times it may be possible to use just floral tape to secure the supporting wire to the stem.

EXTERNAL WIRING II

Broad leaves may need to be bent as well. A loop of wire is placed against the back of the leaf, with the ends of the wire running along the stem. One long end serves to support the stem while the other is wound round both the supporting wire and the stem (see above method). At times, it may be necessary to tape the loop of wire to the leaf surface with a vinyl tape. Make sure the surface of the leaf is dry before doing this.

INTERNAL WIRING

This is an aesthetic method to conceal the wire. Thicker and heavier stems require thicker wires to be inserted into the stems. Hollow stems are easiest but this method can also be used for non-hollow stems. Wires are inserted up to a distance beyond the point to be bent.

EXTERNAL WIRING I

EXTERNAL WIRING II

INTERNAL WIRING

Holding Stems

Holding and securing the stems in place is one of the important fundamentals in ikebana. Various methods have developed and there is no one absolute, correct method.

As long as the stems stay in place, they have access to water and if the method is well-camouflaged, it is the correct way.

In the early days, heavy stones with holes and metal structures with trappings were used. Another common method then was the use of forked twigs and cross-pieces (made of wooden twigs) in the vases to secure the stems (see photo on extreme left).

Stems are sometimes fractured (not separated) at the end and inserted into the vase with the fractured end intact. The fractured end will "open up" and brace itself against the inner wall of the vase (see centre photo). This is especially useful for vases that have narrow mouths.

A variant of this method is to secure a length of wire to the end of the stem and bend the excess wire upwards (see photo on extreme right). This works like the fractured end of the stem in the previous method. You can also coil some wire into a mesh and place it at the mouth of the vase. This ensures that the stems are properly secured when you insert the stems into the mesh.

Kenzans or "pin-holders" are used in containers that have wide, open mouths. They come in various sizes and are for different materials—grass, branches or a combination of both. Plastic *kenzans* are also available and can be used in clear glass containers if they are not too visible. The general rule is that a suitable *kenzan* should be heavy enough (stable) to support the stems that are to be used for the arrangement (see the photo on extreme left).

Floral foam or "oasis", commonly used by florists, is an extremely convenient alternative, provided its limitations are understood. For example, the size and weight of materials to be used with the foam have to be taken into account to ensure sufficient support. Available in large blocks, floral foam can be trimmed to fit into moderate-sized openings. Soak the foam thoroughly in water before trimming and use. Floral foam is also available in hemispherical and other shapes, with double-sided tape on the flat side. This is very convenient when arranging flowers on flat surfaces like a plate. The foam serves to hold as well as to provide the materials with water. Keep the foam constantly wet to ensure that the flowers and leaves last longer. (Note the photos in the centre and on the extreme right.) Plastic orchid tubes can also be used in the same way. They come in different sizes and can be taped or wired to a flat surface.

The Fundamental Considerations

Colour, Shape and Quality

All materials, living and non-living, have colour, shape and a unique quality. Different colours, shapes and qualities suggest different feelings, moods and impressions. Understanding these fundamentals and how they interact with each other will determine the success of your arrangement. Success is achieved when you are able to communicate your thoughts, ideas and feelings to the viewer through your ikebana arrangement. A painter uses various medium, be it charcoal, oils or water colour to portray a scene, a mood or even a person. A songwriter uses music and lyrics to move his listeners. An ikebana practitioner is tasked with the responsibility of orchestrating and coordinating flowers, leaves and accessories, if needed, to convey the mood for the occasion.

Colour

Colour reflects and affects moods and feelings. It should be one of your most important considerations when you select materials for an arrangement. Here are some generally accepted associations:

White is associated with purity.

Black is associated with solemnity.

Gray is associated with modesty and, like white and black, is a quiet colour.

Red is associated with passion and boldness.

Orange is associated with bravery and, like red, evokes a strong emotion.

Yellow is associated with cheeriness and high spirits.

Green is associated with tranquility and, in ikebana, is also known as the "colour of life". A very important colour that is rarely omitted in an arrangement, it plays a vital role in bringing the other colours closer together.

Blue is associated with coolness and is a colour that is easy on the eyes.

Purple is associated with royalty and nobility.

Brown is associated with a sense of stability and reliability.

It is important to note that these are generalizations and that when different colours come together, they may well evoke a completely different feeling altogether.

Shape

Like colours, different shapes hint at a variety of emotions. In freestyle arrangements, you can use the natural form or shape of, for example, the leaf or you can modify its shape to convey a new feeling.

As a guide

- Square represents solidness. It can also be artistic.
- Triangle, with its sharp corners, represents movement, dynamism and is dramatic. It can be elegant too.
- Round represents completeness and conveys a happy feeling, well-suited for a joyous occasion.
- Rectangle represents stability if horizontal, and strength, if vertical. When slanted, it is very dynamic.
- Oval represents grace and elegance.

As a general rule, for a sense of contrast and variation, two vastly different shapes should not be employed in the same arrangement unless one shape serves as the dominant one and the other is less prominent. This helps to achieve harmony.

Quality

This refers to the texture and character of the material. All plant materials have their own unique texture and character. Different surface designs can convey a myriad of emotions.

A leaf with a smooth and shiny texture conveys a sense of lightness and coolness whereas one that is rough, corrugated or hairy has a heavy and strong but duller feel.

A surface that is solid and complete without any "holes" (like the money plant) projects a strong image. A leaf that has spaces between its leaf blades (like the palm leaf) conveys a more graceful and delicate feeling.

A flower such as the gerbera ("daisy") presents itself as a surface, a two-dimensional material, while a lily presents itself as a three-dimensional material, possessing depth and volume.

Some flowers, like the cattelya orchid, are exotic and draw your attention to a focal point while others, like baby's breath, draw your attention to the delicate beauty and add lightness to the arrangement.

Non-plant materials can be modified to send out different impressions. For example, ribbon foil which is linear can be coiled into a mass to give an impression of volume.

The Materials

Accessories, Vases, Equipment

Materials in ikebana arrangements include living materials such as flowers, leaves, branches and even fruits, as well as non-living materials such as bleached or dried floral materials, plastic, paper, fabric, metal sheets, wires and the vase or container. The vase, like the other materials, should be carefully considered for its colour, shape and quality.

Materials can be used in their natural, original state or they can be modified to create a fresh and new impression. A leaf with a broad surface, like the palm leaf, may be trimmed into various shapes to suggest a new image. A plain, light-coloured vase may be transformed by simply pasting coloured ribbon or stickers to enhance its quality. When materials are modified, it must be for a more aesthetic end and not for the sole purpose of modification. Where living materials are concerned, consideration must be given to the water supply to keep them going.

Many of the accessories, vases and equipment can be found in speciality ikebana stores, florist supply centres, the neighbourhood hardware stores, DIY stores or home improvement stores. When you next visit any of these neighbourhood outlets, keep your mind open and look out for possible materials for your next arrangement. All the materials used in this book are from an ikebana resource centre, regular DIY stores and home improvement centres.

1 Cycas fern in its natural state. A delicate feeling.

2 Cycas fern modified by removing some leaf blades along the stem. An artistic impression.

3 Cycas fern modified by removing leaf blades on one side and trimming the other side to form a triangle. A very strong and dynamic impression.

MODIFICATION TO VASES

1 An ordinary looking, plain glass.

2 The glass is transformed by having ribbon foil placed in it. This gives it a new dimension.

3 Here, the transformation is made by attaching coloured plastic "crystals" to the outer surface of the glass, using a glue gun. The glass comes alive with a sparkle.

Ikenobo Ikebana Resource Centre:
Nihon Kado-Sha Co Ltd
Fax: 81-75-212-0659
Ikenobo website: www.ikenobo.or.jp

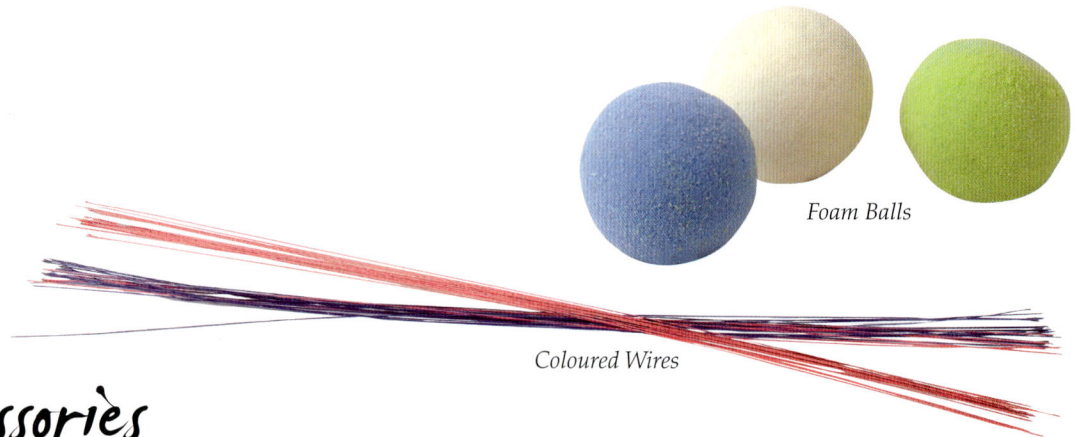

Foam Balls

Coloured Wires

Accessories

The role that accessories play varies with each arrangement. In one, they may complement the flowers and branches and in another, they may lead the arrangement and form the framework. In yet other instances, because of their special quality, accessories may be used as the vase or container for the arrangement, for example, orchid holders to contain the water. Almost anything can be used as an accessory and the following is not an exhaustive list :

Rattan Balls

Feather

Plastic "Crystals"

Ribbon Foil

Fancy Paper

Fancy Paper

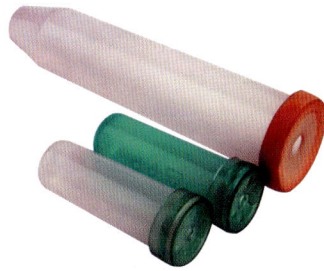

Orchid Holders

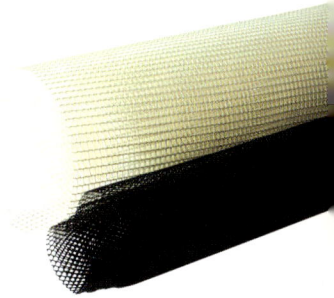

Plastic Gardening Mesh

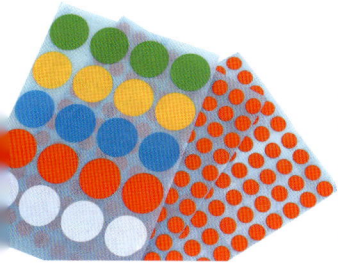

Stickers

Garden Mesh

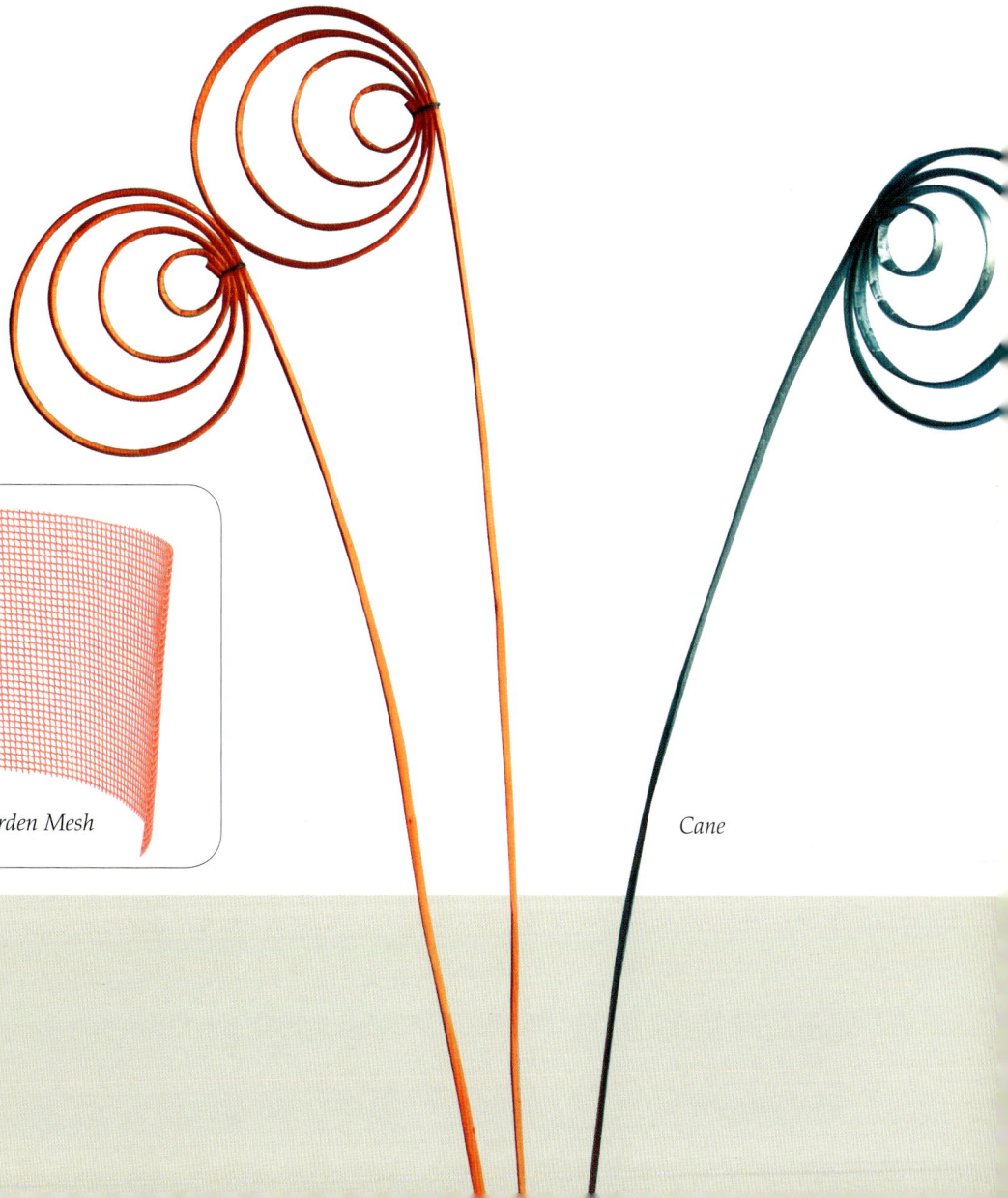

Cane

Vases

A wide variety of vases can be used for ikebana.

Broadly classified into three groups, they are as follows:

Traditional ikebana vases

These vases can be used for any style, from the very traditional rikka to the very modern freestyle. As *kenzans* are usually used in traditional arrangements, the mouths of these vases are wide. And because these vases taper towards the base, they help to make the arrangements look more elegant.

Abstract freestyle vases

These vases usually have irregular shapes. *Kenzans* are traditionally used to hold the materials in place but because the mouths of these vases are normally small and irregular, other means of holding the materials are employed.

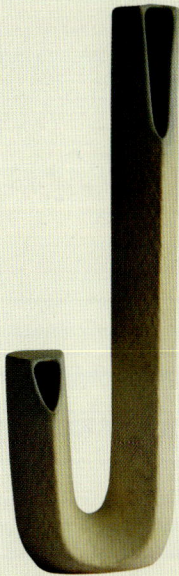

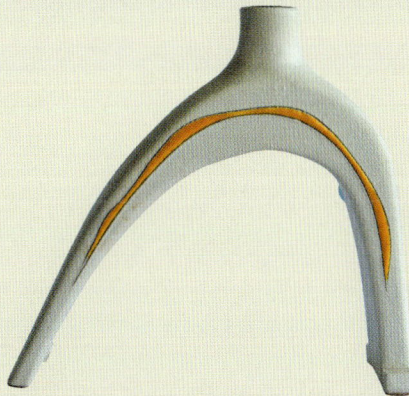

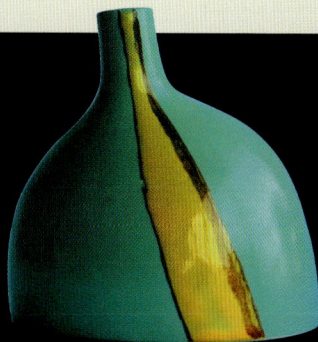

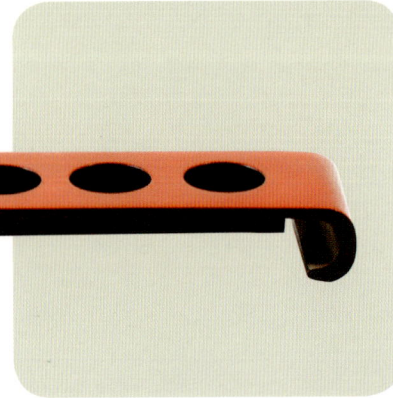

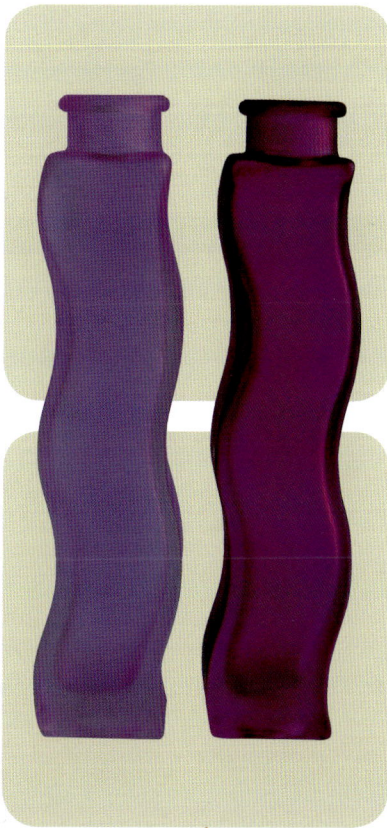

Others

With a little bit of imagination, a dash of creativity and a sound understanding of how to hold and provide water for the materials, you can transform anything—from a common household utensil to crockery—into the ideal vase for the perfect ikebana arrangement.

Equipment

Floral tape

Floral tape that comes in a variety of colours, ranging from white, to various shades of green, brown and other colours, serves to camouflage the wired stems and at times, to secure the wire to the stems.

Stem tape

This is not common. Stem tapes are special cotton tapes used in Ikenobo ikebana and sold in shades of green and brown. Wrap them around a separated stem, from the point of separation to the end that is immersed in water. The fabric helps to draw water from the source to the separated part, hence prolonging the life of the stem. These tapes can also be used to lengthen or increase the height of an otherwise very short material. To do this, attach any healthy stem of about the same diameter to the material to give the extra length or height required and camouflage with the tape.

Various types of tapes are available in the market.

Vinyl and other tape

Vinyl tape, such as your regular transparent tape and the coloured electrician's tape, is strong and slightly elastic. Use this to secure thicker wires to branches before camouflaging with floral tape. Double-sided tape comes in handy when you need to stick two surfaces together.

Tools

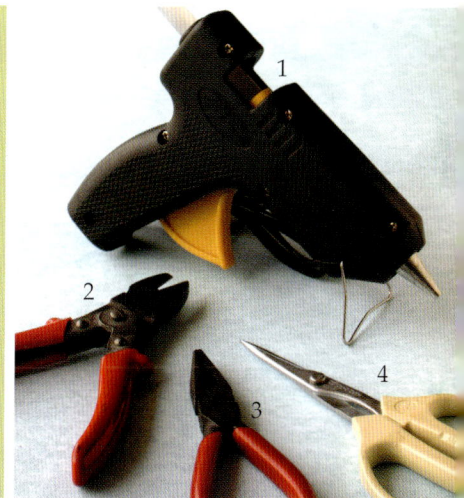

1 Glue gun
   This very useful tool is used when you need to attach any material that has an uneven surface, like a piece of plastic crystal, to another surface.

2 Wire cutter

3 Pliers

4 Scissors

Wires

Various thicknesses of wires are available and these are denoted by even numbers (14, 16, 18, etc). A smaller number denotes a thicker wire. The choice of wires used depends on the strength and weight of the stems to be bent. Use thicker wires to support the bends of heavier branches and to thread through the stems so that the bends are supported aesthetically.

Wires are available in silver, black or wrapped in different coloured floral tapes. Choose a colour that closely matches the colour of the stem.

Freestyle in Three Movements

All living things move—movement is a sign of life. In ikebana which stresses the importance of life, movement, no matter how subtle, must be evident in the completed arrangement. In Ikenobo freestyle, you are free to choose the movement characterised in the basic vertical, horizontal and slanting forms.

The vertical form represents solemnity, strength and hope and is the most appropriate for formal events like the New Year. The horizontal form has a more relaxed and laid-back feeling to it. It is less "energetic" compared to the other two. The slanting form is stylish and dynamic and scores high for its movement content compared to the vertical or horizontal forms.

In this chapter, you will learn the principles in freestyle through these three basic forms. You will also learn their associated movements and ways to bring out these movements.

Vertical 1

Gerbera, Sword Fern, Heliconia, Black Mountain Grass, Dendrobium Orchid

1 Yellow gerberas are randomly arranged in a vertical fashion. Sword ferns are placed, facing the front at the base, to anchor the arrangement.

2 The red heliconia further anchors the upward movement of the gerberas.

3 Black mountain grass adds texture and colour contrast.

4 A single bloom of dendrobium acts as a focal point and completes the arrangement.

Vertical 2

Viburnum, Strelitzia, Philodendron, Hypericum, White Phoenix

1 Viburnum stands proud, forming the vertical framework.

2 Strelitzia anchors and adds contrast to the base on one side while the fresh green surface of the philodendron provides a refreshing contrast on the other side.

3 Hypericum enhances the upward movement as well as anchors the arrangement.

4 White phoenix completes the arrangement by providing a delicate yet striking focus.

49

Vertical 3

Sanseviera, Rose, Heliconia, Yellow Phoenix, Hypericum

1 The beautiful surfaces of the sanseviera leaves are arranged in two groups, in a vertical fashion.

2 A red rose is placed at the base of the larger group. The rose very beautifully contrasts with the white vase and acts as a point of interest.

3 Heliconia anchors and gives contrast to the smaller group while the phoenix adds lightness to contrast with the red rose.

4 Hypericum contrasts with the heliconia and adds the finishing touch.

Vertical 4

Strelitzia, Palm, White Phoenix

1 Strelitzias are placed in different postures but with a similar movement in a basin-type vase.

2 Two palm leaves with most of their leaf blades removed are added to lighten and create some movement.

3 A small palm is added on the other side to balance the larger palm leaf while a short stem of the phoenix adds depth and colour contrast.

4 Phoenix is added in the front as a focus and to bring out the upward movement.

Horizontal 1

Snake grass, Strelitzia, Euphorbia, Dendrobium Orchid, Calathea

1 Size #20 wires are inserted into the stems of the snake grass which are then bent and placed horizontally.

2 Two stems of strelitzia are placed in the centre of the arrangement, providing a colourful starting point for the horizontally extending snake grass.

3 Euphorbia extends forward, adding colour and textural contrast.

4 A single bloom of the dendrobium adds focus. The maroon calathea leaves are placed at the rear to bring out the colours of the flowers and to add depth to the arrangement.

Horizontal 2

Anthurium, Lisianthus, Philodendron, Heliconia, Purple Phoenix

1 Anthuriums are placed horizontally in an asymmetrical fashion.

2 Two stems of lisianthus are added in the centre at the base for colour contrast.

3 The lime-coloured philodendron leaves add a nice contrast and harmonize with the movement of the anthuriums.

4 The heliconia, extending to the front on the left, provides textural contrast while the one in the rear adds a sense of depth. The single, delicate purple phoenix acts as a focus.

Horizontal 3

Vanda Orchid, Sword Fern, Baby's Breath, Freesia

1 Stems of vanda are braced against each other in the irregular mouth of the vase. The colour of the vanda contrasts beautifully with the vase.

2 Sword ferns are modified to create lightness and they enhance the horizontal movement.

3 Baby's breath further lightens the mood and adds colour contrast.

4 Yellow freesia is added for textural and colour contrast.

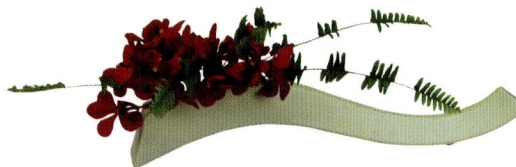

Slanting 1

Snake Grass, Lisianthus, Euphorbia, Coconut Leaves

1 Floral foam is used to hold the materials in this vase which has a narrow mouth. Size #20 wires are inserted into the stems to support the snake grass. Several stems of snake grass are bent and angulated to the right, forming the slanting framework.

2 Lisianthus anchors the movement of the snake grass while providing a refreshing contrast in colour and form.

3 Euphorbia is placed next to the lisianthus and adds textural contrast.

4 Two coconut leaves are wired and angled in the same way as the snake grass to enhance the movement as well as to provide a contrast with the snake grass.

Slanting 2

Black Mountain Grass, Coconut Leaves, Rose

1 Stalks of black mountain grass are freely arranged at an angle to the left in a slanting fashion.

2 Two coconut leaves are curved and wired to the grass, enhancing the slanting movement of the grass. They provide a beautiful colour contrast with the grass and vase.

3 Two roses in full bloom anchor the movement of the grass.

4 More grass is added to heighten the colour contrast with the coconut leaves.

Slanting 3

Coloured cane, Rose, Coconut leaves

1 Coloured canes act as the main material to form the framework of the arrangement.

2 A purple rose at the base nicely contrasts with the white vase and yellow cane and anchors the movement of the cane.

3 Another stem of rose is used tall to accompany the yellow cane.

4 Coconut leaves are placed amidst the yellow cane and rose for colour and textural contrast.

Seeing in New Light

While it is possible for an arrangement to focus on the overall beauty of floral materials, almost invariably, it is more dramatic and refreshing to focus on the beauty of the various components of the materials.

This involves changing the way you look at flowers, leaves and accessories and learning to examine them as possessing one or more of the following components.

Line

Most materials possess line in the form of the stems or leaves (like the long leaves of the coconut leaves, and iris leaves). Some of these stems have interesting colours or design that can serve as the focus of the arrangement.

Line functions in a variety of ways; they give a sense of direction, divide spaces and lighten the mood of the arrangement.

Lines that are straight give a sharp, energetic impression while a curved line is softer and lighter in feeling. Jagged lines give a heavier impression.

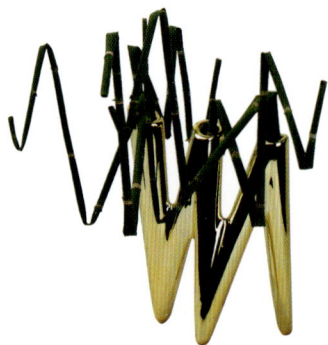

Line 1

Snake Grass, Baby's Breath, Heliconia, Dendrobium Orchid

1 Size #20 wires are inserted into the stems of the snake grass which are bent in a zig-zag manner to mimic the vase.

2 Baby's breath is added to soften the mood.

3 A single bloom of dendrobium adds focus.

4 A red heliconia, added towards the rear for colour and textural contrast, completes the arrangement.

Line 2

Coconut Leaves, Craspedia, Gloriosa, Philodendron, Vanda Orchid

1 The stems of two coconut leaves, secured at their ends by a craspedia, are wired with size #24 wire to form a window. Another two stems arch to the left for balance.

2 Gloriosa adds colour contrast and acts as an anchor for the arrangement.

3 Philodendron introduces a much needed refreshing surface to the arrangement.

4 Two stems of the craspedia add movement and enhance the window created by the coconut leaves. A purple vanda sits at the rear for depth and colour contrast.

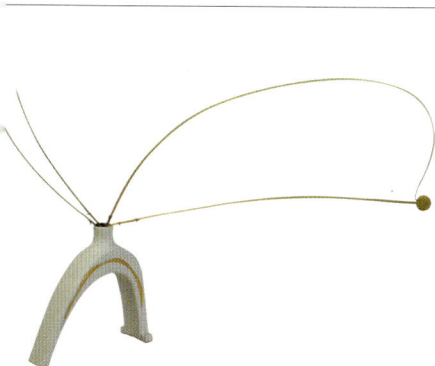

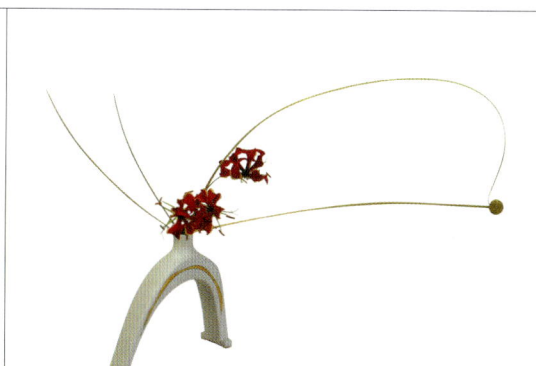

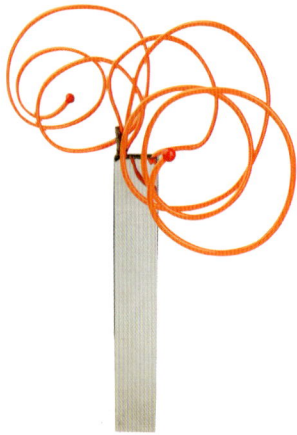

Line 3

Coloured Wire, Sword Fern, Vanda Orchid, Baby's Breath

1 Orange coloured wire is placed in a tall stainless steel vase. The design of the wire gives a strong contrast to the vase.

2 The modified leaves are wired with size #26 wires to the coloured wires to enhance the circular movement.

3 A red orchid is added to the centre of the arrangement and this adds a point of interest.

4 Baby's breath is added to give colour contrast and to soften the arrangement.

Line 4

Coloured Wire, Ribbon Foil, Feather, Rose, Fern

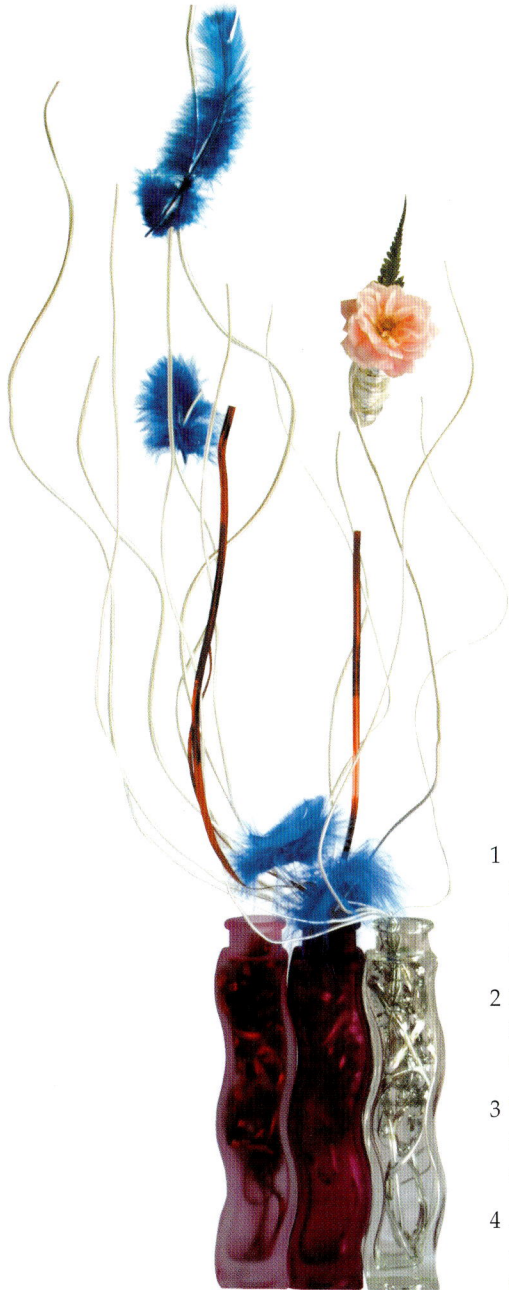

1. A vertical framework of silver wires is formed to replicate the shape of the vases. An orchid holder is camouflaged with silver ribbon foil and secured at the top.

2. Blue feathers are secured to various points in the silver framework for colour and textural contrast.

3. Two strips of red ribbon foil are added to further enhance the harmony between arrangement and vase.

4. A pink rose and fern are placed into the orchid holder filled with water, to complete this modern freestyle arrangement.

Surface

Surfaces are usually associated with leaf surfaces and large surface-type flowers like the sunflower. Such surfaces can be longish, oval or round in their natural state but they can also be modified into new shapes to give them a refreshing change in appearance and feeling.

When many lines are placed next to one another, a surface is also formed. The surface functions to provide strength and a background. When two or more are used, they can add a sense of rhythm, depth and three-dimensionality.

Surface 1

Monstera, Lily, Craspedia, Statice

1 Two large monstera leaves are placed to show their lush green surfaces. The plain vase is modified by gluing two craspedia to the vase.

2 Two lilies are placed in front of one of the leaves and their colour and form are enhanced by the leaves.

3 Purple statice lends a beautiful contrast to the monstera.

4 Two stems of craspedia are added to enhance the contrast and work in harmony with the modified vase.

Surface 2

Money Plant, Freesia, Strelitzia, White Phoenix

1 The money plant leaves of various sizes are arranged front to rear, displaying their beautifully variegated surfaces as well as suggesting movement. A stem of freesia anchors the arrangement at the base.

2 More freesia are added to enhance their delicateness and to create new spaces.

3 Strelitzia adds colour contrast and further strengthens the base in the rear.

4 Two blooms of the phoenix add colour and contrast in form.

Surface 3

Palm, Gerbera, Money Plant, Oncidium Orchid

1 The palm leaves are modified to create a light feeling.

2 Red gerberas are positioned at the top to contrast with the palm leaves and at the base to anchor the arrangement.

3 A variegated money plant leaf is placed at the rear to add contrast and depth.

4 A delicate stem of bright oncidium gives colour and textural contrast.

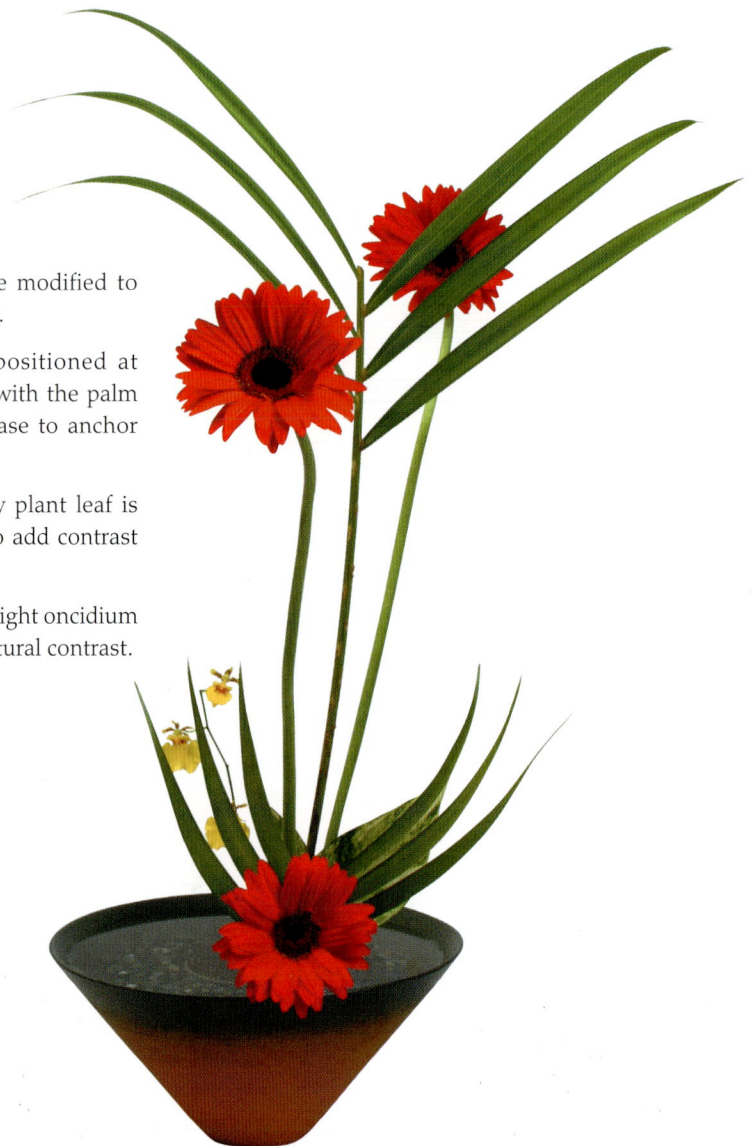

Surface 4

Monstera, Cymbidium Orchid, Statice, Coconut Leaves

1 Three monstera leaves are modified into rectangles of different sizes, with the largest right in front and the smallest at the rear to create depth. The stems of the leaves have been wired with size #18 wires. Floral foam is used to hold the materials in the vase.

2 A cymbidium is placed in front at the base, and its perfect form and colour is enhanced by the intense green of the monstera. Another stalk of cymbidium peeks from behind at the upper level.

3 Purple statice is added to heighten the colour and textural contrast.

4 To give a sense of direction, two coconut leaves are added. They serve to contrast in colour and shape with the monstera leaves.

Point

Points usually refer to small flowers that may be found on a single stem like the narcissus, or in a cluster like baby's breath. Due to their nature, points usually add a feeling of lightness to an arrangement. They also suggest movement in a subtle way. When small flowers are used in a single area, they serve as a focal point or point of interest for the arrangement.

Point 1

Caspia, Palm, Rose, Money Plant

1 Several stems of caspia are freely arranged and held in place by a plastic stem holder in the clear glass vase.

2 A palm leaf, modified with most of its leaf blades removed, is placed amidst the caspia, providing colour and textural contrast.

3 A pink rose is added as a focus for the arrangement.

4 A small money plant leaf is placed at the rear for contrast and balance.

Point 2

Plastic Gardening Mesh, Stickers, Coconut Leaf, Baby's Breath, Purple Phoenix

1 Black plastic mesh is rolled and wired to the vase with size #18 wire. Coloured stickers are pasted at random, forming a fun and colourful framework.

2 A coconut leaf is wired with size #22 wire and bent to give the arrangement its movement. It is placed in a small orchid holder embedded in the mesh.

3 Baby's breath is lightly arranged to enhance the theme of points and for colour contrast.

4 A single bloom of purple phoenix completes this arrangement emphasizing the beauty of points.

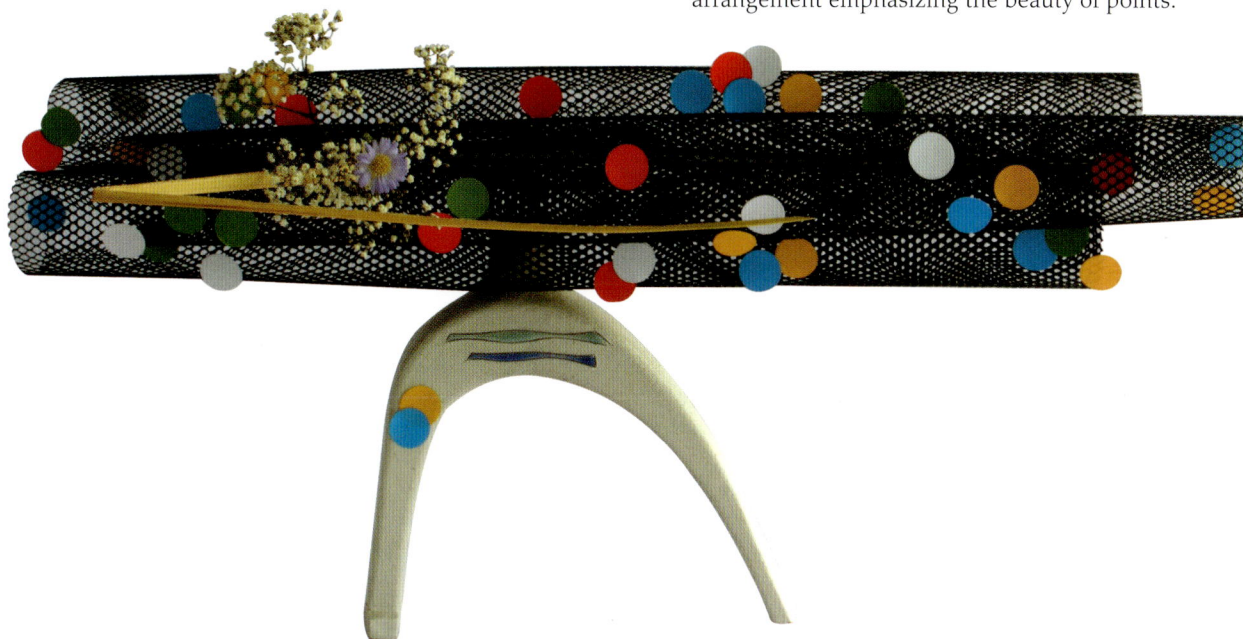

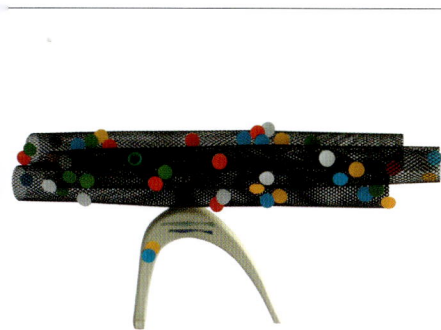

Point 3

Queen Anne's Lace, Rose, Purple Phoenix, Pittosporum, Philodendron

1 Several stems of Queen Anne's lace are placed freely in the two mouths of the vase. The stems are wired with size #22 wires.

2 A red rose sits pretty at the mouth on the right and its concentrated form contrasts well with the lace flowers.

3 More lace flowers are added to ground the movement of the lace flowers while a purple phoenix adds focus.

4 A philodendron leaf gives a sharp contrast to the lace flowers on the left while the variegated pittosporum leaf lightens the right side of the arrangement.

Point 4

Ribbon Foil, Misty Pink, Eryngium, Oncidium Orchid

1 Four glass vases are used with two in an inverted position. Silver ribbon foil is placed in the two vases and extends out of the vases to form a network.

2 Misty pink is added to form an airy mass of small pink flowers. The ribbon foil supports and adds sparkle.

3 The dark purple eryngium flowers add focus.

4 A very delicate but bright stem of the oncidium orchid provides contrast to the dark purple eryngium.

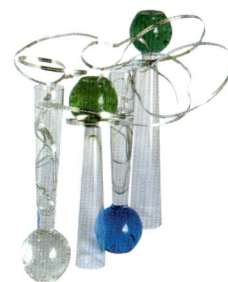

Mass

This term refers to flowers in clusters or efflorescence like hydrangea and celosia (cockscomb). When many points come together, they form a mass. Non-flowering materials like the asparagus fern also have a mass or volume effect.

Arrangements with mass materials can be very bold and avant garde. Since the materials are voluminous in nature, they convey a three-dimensional effect. At the same time, although concentrated and heavy in feeling, they suggest movement when used in varying densities in an arrangement.

Mass 1

Vanda Orchid, Coconut Leaf, Sanseviera, Craspedia

1 A cluster of red vanda orchids is placed in the silver vase forming a lovely mass.

2 Two sanseviera leaves emerge to add visual weight to the rear.

3 Two craspedia tucked in near the sanseviera leaves anchor the movement.

4 A coconut leaf is wired with size #22 wire and arches above the orchid cluster, introducing movement and contrast in colour and form to the arrangement.

Mass 2

Gerbera, Sanseviera, Yellow Phoenix, Euphorbia

1 The vibrant gerberas are placed close to one another to form a horizontal mass.

2 Sanseviera leaves are added to the rear for colour and textural contrast.

3 Yellow phoenix is added next to the "hard" sanseviera leaves for textural and colour contrast.

4 Euphorbia further lightens the arrangement while a yellow gerbera, with its outer petals removed, adds a subtle variation.

Mass 3

Hydrangea, Gerbera, Rattan Ball, Hypericum, Coconut Leaf

1 The form of the hydrangea flowers matches the vase to a tee.

2 A yellow gerbera adds colour and textural contrast to the globular mass of flowers.

3 Further textural contrast is provided by the silver rattan balls wired together with size #24 wire. A small cluster of the hypericum's red points adds an interesting contrast.

4 A coconut leaf is wired with size #22 wire and arches over the arrangement. This defines an interesting space for the flowers and brings movement into an otherwise static arrangement

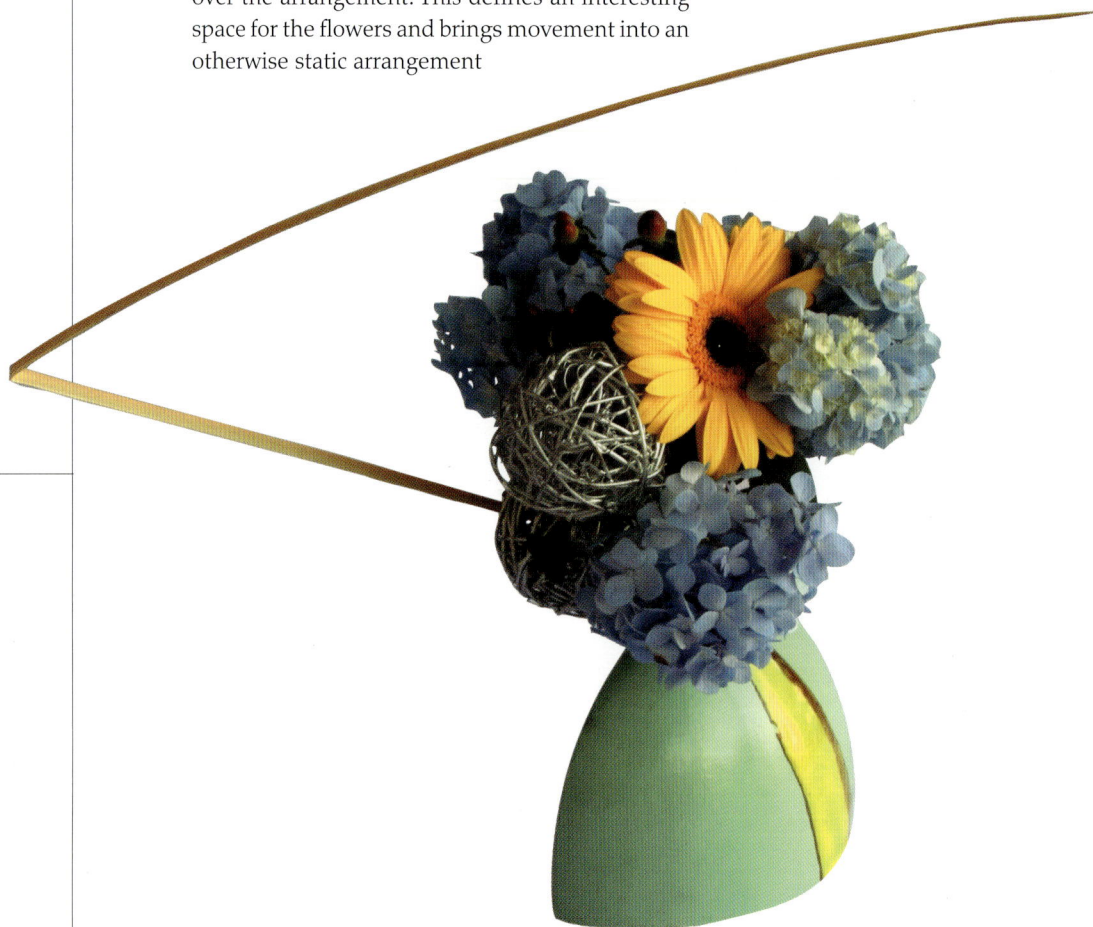

Mass 4

Lily, Anthurium, Queen Anne's Lace, Hypericum

1 A few lilies are placed in the vase with the help of size #20 wires.

2 An unusually large and beautiful two-toned anthurium brings out the perfect form of the white lilies.

3 The delicate lace flowers are added to soften the contrast between the strong flowers used.

4 The fine red points of the hypericum help to add colour and textural contrast.

Any Vase
Will Do

The vase is much more than just a vessel to contain water. Very often, it can be the source of inspiration for an arrangement. Look around you and, depending on your creativity, you can find almost any article in the home or office that can be used as an interesting vase or container for a freestyle arrangement.

It is therefore vital to consider the colour, shape and quality of the vase first and then the floral materials and accessories that would best bring out the beauty of the vase.

This chapter takes a look at the use of non-traditional vases.

Arrangement 1

Leather Bag, Delphinium, Yellow Phoenix, Anthurium, Coconut Leaves

1 Five stems of delphinium are arranged in random fashion, standing tall in the leather bag filled with floral foam.

2 Yellow phoenix are placed at the base of the arrangement to provide contrast and camouflage the floral foam.

3 A stem of anthurium is placed at the rear, on the left, behind the yellow phoenix. It is only partially seen, thus adding a subtle focus.

4 Two blades of the coconut leaves on the left rise to give direction and adds sharpness to the whole arrangement.

Arrangement 2

Crystal Ashtray, Nerine Lily, Muraya Leaves, Anthurium, Ming Fern,
Dendrobium Orchid, Black Mountain Grass

1 Three nerine lilies stand tall in the ashtray filled with floral foam.

2 A shorter muraya leaf anchors the base while the taller one meanders across the lilies upwards.

3 An anthurium is placed low on the left to further anchor the arrangement while a taller one facing backwards stands tall supporting the upward movement. Ming fern at the base camouflages the floral foam and adds textural contrast to the arrangement.

4 Two black mountain grass stands at the rear to further enhance the upward movement while a few blooms of dendrobium orchids adds colour contrast to the arrangement at the base and completes the arrangement.

Arrangement 3

Chinese Wine Bottle, Plastic Mesh, Oncidium Orchid, Ming Fern, Dendrobium Orchid

1 Bend a piece of red plastic gardening mesh into a curve by threading two size #16 wires (wrapped in red floral tape) through it and anchor it into the Chinese wine bottle.

2 A stem of oncidium is placed into the bottle through the mesh at an angle

3 A stem of Ming fern is then placed into the bottle making sure that the leaves in the lower part of the stem hide the mouth of the bottle

4 A white dendrobium orchid sits pretty in the centre bringing focus and contrast to the whole arrangement.

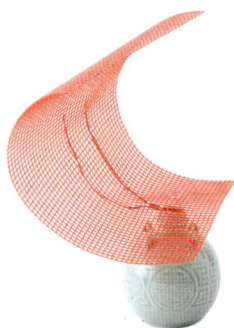

Arrangement 4

Tea-light Holder, Coloured Floral Foam Balls, Palm Leaves, Heliconia, Polyscias

1 Blue and beige foam balls are placed onto the five openings on the tea-light holder. Two palm leaves, modified by cutting the tip and the lower blades, are inserted into the extreme right two foam balls in an upright manner.

2 Another two palm leaves modified in the same manner are inserted, one tall and the other shorter, at the base of the extreme left foam ball.

3 An open heliconia flower anchors the movement of the leaves in the extreme left while a heliconia bud is inserted adjacent to the second last foam ball on the right, enhancing the upward movement.

4 A polyscias leaf placed behind the heliconia flower on the left adds contrast in form and colour while another pair of the polyscias leaves anchors the heliconia bud on the right.

Arrangement 5

Sauce Container, Pin-cushion, Milky Bush, Capsicum, Finger Palm, Coconut Leaf

1 Two stems of pin-cushion flowers are inserted facing forwards into the sauce container filled with floral foam.

2 Milky bush are added to form a semi-circular shape.

3 A finger palm enhances the overall shape while the capsicum adds focus.

4 A blade of coconut leaf arches forwards from the rear adding lightness and variation.

Arrangement 6

Lacquer Tissue Box Holder, Orchids, Fruticosus, Gerbera, Capsicum, Fern Leaves

1 The lacquer tissue box is filled with floral foam. Red orchids are randomly inserted in a horizontal fashion camouflaging the opening.

2 Several stems of fruticosus are arranged in an upright and slanting fashion.

3 A yellow gerbera is tucked in the lower right rear adding a subtle contrast.

4 Capsicum flower is placed in the front left to add focus.

5 Three stems of fern leaves, with many of the leaflets removed, adds lightness and depth to the arrangement in an enclosing fashion.

Arrangement 7

Cookie Tin, Money Plant, Spathiphyllum, Gerbera, Ming Fern, Anthurium, Cordyline

1 Several money plant leaves are inserted into the floral foam-filled cookie tin facing forwards and upwards, creating a mass of green filling the tin.

2 Three stems of spathiphyllum are arranged in an upright fashion on the left, facing forwards.

3 Two stems of gerberas are arranged on the right, also facing forward contrasting with the form and colours of the spathiphyllum while the Ming fern adds a textural contrast to the base of the arrangement.

4 A pink anthurium is positioned at the left rear while the three blades of the cordyline leaves intersperse with the flowers to enhance the upward movement of the arrangement.

Arrangement 8

Watering Can, Muraya Leaves, Gerberas, Spathyphillum, Heliconia

1 Muraya leaves are randomly placed in the watering can, extending horizontally.

2 Pink gerberas are also randomly placed in the centre providing beautiful contrast against the leaves.

3 Two stems of white spathyphillum flowers are placed in the centre, at the rear, while two stems of heliconia are placed on the front left heightening the contrast in the whole arrangement.

4 A yellow gerbera is tucked in the left rear acting as a focal point for the whole arrangement.

93

Arrangement 9

Cow Soup Bowl And Saucer, Hydrangea, Pin-Cushion, Onion Leaves

1 A bright yellow hydrangea sits pretty in the bowl almost occupying the whole mouth.

2 Two stems of pin-cushion are added at the rear right to give colour and textural contrast. No special mechanics are employed here as the flowers are held in place by bracing against each other.

3 A bunch of onion leaves adds lightness and completes the arrangement.

Arrangement 10

Salad Bowl, Coloured Floral Foam Balls, Coloured Acrylic Pebbles, Pineapple Leaves, Mini-roses, Capsicum, Wax Flower

1 Green floral foam balls are anchored into the rim of the salad bowl on either side. Blades of pineapple leaves are inserted in each ball and made to cross to the opposite side in an asymmetrical fashion. Coloured pebbles are placed in the bowl with some water to create a reflective effect in the bowl, adding dimension.

2 Pink mini-roses are inserted in the rear foam ball.

3 Capsicum flower is added beside the mini-roses to give contrast while another is placed in the foam ball in front.

4 Wax flower is placed behind the front capsicum flower, adding colour to the whole arrangement.

Arrangement 11

Tea-light Stands, Peacock Flower, Cymbidium Orchid, Schefflera, Ming Fern, Dendrobium Orchid

1 The taller tea-light holder is placed diagonally in front of the shorter one. A stem of the peacock flower with a sensuous curve in the taller front stand. Floral foam fills the mouth of the holders.

2 A second stem of the peacock flower with a generous curve further accentuates the movement of the first adding drama against the two upright holders.

3 A third peacock flower is placed angling to to front left while a cymbidium orchid rests on the shorter holder in the rear.

4 Schefflera leaves are placed as background to the arrangements in both the holders.

5 Ming fern in the heart of the taller arrangement adds textural contrast while in the lower arrangement adds softness and depth beyond the schefflera leaf. Finally, a white dendrobium orchid adds a soft touch to the whole arrangement in the upper rear.

That Special Moment

When fairy lights, Santa Claus figures, reindeers and tassles of red, green and gold deck the shopping malls and the city streets, we know it is Christmas. It is the same with ikebana. When certain floral materials and accessories are used in an arrangement, we are reminded of a particular event, occasion or festival.

Ikebana, in addition to this, addresses the viewer on a more personal level. An arrangement can bring to mind special memories like when the wedding proposal was made over a candle-lit dinner and a bouquet of roses. Precious moments shared come alive once more.

Palm Sunday

Lily, Palm, Money Plant, Hypericum, Coconut Leaf

1 Two lilies, with most of their leaves and buds removed, lean elegantly to the right.

2 Two red palms with one side of their leaves removed serve as a background.

3 A variegated money plant leaf is added at the base to anchor the movement and partially camouflage the *kenzan*. Another palm adds an interesting variation.

4 A coconut leaf brightens up the arrangement while the hypericum adds focus.

The Proposal

Candle Stands, Candles, Rose, Astilbe, Carthamus, Zig-zag

1 Floral foam fills the candle stands and the candles are wedged into the foam. White roses are added to the base of the candles.

2 Astilbe is added for a subtle variation.

3 The striking carthamus is added to heighten the contrast.

4 Zig-zag, sprayed gold, forms a beautiful network linking the two candle stands and adding life to the arrangement.

101

Mother's Day

Plastic Crystals, Card, Lily, Yellow Phoenix, Carnation, Calathea

1 Plastic crystals are glued to the slender glass vase. Floral foam, wrapped in aluminium foil, is wedged into the narrow mouth of the vase. A beautiful lily sits pretty and crowns the vase.

2 Yellow phoenix forms the background for the lily and adds textural contrast.

3 A pink carnation peeks out at the side, amidst the phoenix.

4 The rich surface of the calathea enhances the colour and form of the lily and completes this floral tribute to mothers.

Trick or Treat

Pumpkin Container, Party Hat, Ming Fern, Sunflower, Eryngium, Astilbe

1 Ming fern is inserted into the container, which is filled with floral foam, to form a mass.

2 A party hat is wired to a stem and positioned just above the mass of green to add a festive spirit.

3 Sunflowers add life to the arrangement while the partially hidden eryngium provides depth and contrast.

4 Astilbe adds texture and a much needed colour contrast in this halloween arrangement.

Wedding Anniversary

Vase, Fancy Paper, Oncidium Orchid, Allium, Money Plant

1 Silver and gold fancy paper is cut into squares of various sizes and size #22 wire is taped to the back of the squares.

2 A few stems of oncidium extend from the gold towards the silver area.

3 Purple allium flowers at the rear give depth, add visual weight to the arrangement and harmonize with the colour of the vase.

4 Money plant leaf adds a dash of green to this glitzy arrangement.

Hark! The Herald Angels Sing

Christmas-themed Container, Ribbon Foil, Baby's Breath, Phlox

1 Red ribbon foil is coiled round a thick, size #18 wire that is placed into the container through a hole for the straw.

2 More ribbon coil is added to create a mass.

3 Baby's breath is added in the confines of the mass to give colour and textural contrast.

4 A stem of phlox bearing two pristinely white flowers floats in the sea of red and white, completing this cute Christmas arrangement.

Akemashite Omedetou (Happy New Year)

Rose, Calla Lily, Queen Anne's Lace, Philodendron

1 Red roses form a mass on the left.

2 White calla lilies and a white rose add intense contrast.

3 Queen Anne's lace is added between the red and white and softens the stark contrast.

4 Philodendron leaves sit behind the red roses for depth and bring out the redness of the roses.

Be My Valentine

Heart-shaped Box with Cover, Aluminium Foil, Chocolate, Astilbe, Rose, Misty Pink, Eryngium

1 Wrapped in aluminium foil, the cover conceals the floral foam in the container as it is propped up against a cup at the back. A pair of heart-shaped chocolates is stuck to the silver top. Astilbe forms a shelter.

2 A white rose anchors the movement for the arrangement.

3 Misty pink adds textural contrast and lightens the mood.

4 Purple eryngium further enhances the white rose and adds depth to this Valentine's Day arrangement.

Right At Home

The home is an excellent practice ground for putting your ikebana skills to the test. In practice and reality, arrangements are not always table arrangements as is the usual practice when learning ikebana. Ikebana is so versatile that every nook and corner, any wall, large and wide spaces or tall and narrow spaces, can be enhanced to bring that space to life. In this chapter, we explore two different home environments to highlight the many possibilities of ikebana.

Warm Welcome

Pamper your guests. Make them feel right at home. Let them experience the warmth of your hospitality as you treat them to refreshing surprises on the coffee table, sideboard, console or wall shelves.

Hydrangea, Gerbera, Hypericum, Coconut Leaf, Rattan Balls

Cymbidium Orchid, Dracaena, Hypericum

Raphis Palm, Lily, Hypericum, Golden Shower

*Anthuriums, Pandanus, Yellow Phoenix,
Queen Anne's Lace, Freesia*

Amaranthus, Heliconia, Anthurium, Yellow Phoenix,
Pittosporum, Coconut Leaves

Black Mountain Grass, Lily, Monstera, Golden Shower,
White Phoenix, Hypericum

A Refreshing View

Arrangements may sometimes be complete on its own (this page)
or they may enhance spaces beyond the confines of a room (facing
page), adding new dimensions to the room.

Amaranthus, Freesia, Dendrobium
Orchid, Anethum, Pandanus